The Dragon, the Knight, and the Princess
EDWARD ALAN KURTZ

Paperback • eBook • Audiobook • Soundtrack

Stergiou Limited • 2016

SOUNDTRACK

Composer: David J. Franco

© 2016 Edward Alan Kurtz
All rights reserved

COPYRIGHT

The Dragon, the Knight, and the Princess
© 2016 EDWARD ALAN KURTZ
Images & Illustrations: Adobe Stock

Available in print, eBook and audiobook

ISBN: 978-1-910370-79-7 (Stergiou Limited-Assigned)
ISBN: 978-1533269-47-8 (CreateSpace-Assigned)
ePub ISBN: 978-1-910370-78-0 (Stergiou Limited-Assigned)

Published by Stergiou Limited
Suite A, 6 Honduras Street,
London EC1Y 0TH,
United Kingdom
Email: publications@stergioultd.com
Web: http://stergioultd.com

All rights reserved

Contents

Chapter One	*The Kingdom*	6
Chapter Two	*The Biggest Dragon in the World!*	11
Chapter Three	*A New Start*	16
Chapter Four	*The Start of the Adventure*	22
Chapter Five	*The Magic Lake*	28
Chapter Six	*The Mountain with the Surprise at the Top*	34
Chapter Seven	*Snow!*	39
Chapter Eight	*Trapped!*	44
Chapter Nine	*Return to the Giant Dragon's Cave*	49
Chapter Ten	*Return to the Valley*	54
About the Author	*Edward Alan Kurtz*	59

CHAPTER ONE

The Kingdom

Once upon a time, in a land far away, there was a special kingdom. It was the largest kingdom in the land, and the people who lived there were very happy.

The kingdom sat in a huge valley that was surrounded by mountains. There was a river that flowed though the valley, and this river was important to the people of the kingdom. It gave them water to drink, and they could also use it to water their fields.

The valley was full of fields with many kinds of crops. People grew grains and vegetables. There were even orchards to grow fruit. There were large vineyards to grow grapes.

But, right in the very middle of the valley, right in the middle of the fields, there was something very unusual.

Up from the floor of the valley rose a large, rocky hill, and at the very top of this hill sat a castle. The hill was called Castle Hill. It was where the king and his queen lived.

It was not very easy to get to the castle, because the sides of the rocky hill were very steep. However, a long path wound its way to the top of the hill.

At the bottom of Castle Hill was a big wooden gate that had been built between two huge rocks. Guards would stand in front of the gate to protect the castle at the top of the hill.

If you were allowed to pass through the big wooden gateway, the guards would open it for you, and then close it right away. Now, you would have to be ready to walk round and round on the path that led to the top of Castle Hill.

At the top of the path were large wooden doors. This was the only way into the castle, because it was surrounded by walls. More guards kept watch at these wooden doors. They would open it for you if you needed to see the king.

Once you passed beyond the big wooden doors, you would enter a very large open courtyard. There were many small buildings here. Some of them were attached to the inside of the wall that surrounded the castle, and some of the buildings stood in the courtyard.

There were many people who lived there; their job was to serve the king, so the people were often running around the courtyard, trying to get their jobs done. There were also plenty of animals in the courtyard, especially chickens!

There were buildings and people and animals, but the thing that was easies to see in the courtyard was a very tall and old oak tree. Some people believed it was thousands of years old. No one knew for sure, but there was one thing that everyone knew.

At the trunk of the old oak tree, there was water. No one knew how it got up to the top of Castle Hill, but many years before, someone had built a stone well, and now, there was drinking water for the king and everyone who served him.

Just beyond the tree and the well, the king and his family lived. It was a small family: just the king, his wife, the queen, and their daughter, the princess. Her name was Juliana.

Inside, it was very beautiful. There were many colorful windows, soft rugs, and many rooms. Some of the rooms, such as the bedrooms, were just for the family. Other rooms were used by the king whenever he had meetings with people from his kingdom.

On the other side of the courtyard, near the big wooden doors, was a room where the king's knights lived. One of the knights was very strong and handsome. His name was Sir Roger, and he could do things better than any other knight in the kingdom.

Now, the king was getting old. He and the queen had just one child: Princess Juliana. The king knew how important it was for his daughter to find a good husband. That way, the king would know that the kingdom and all of the people would continue to be happy.

So it was that the king often looked out of his bedroom window when the knights were practicing. What did they practice? They practiced fighting each other so that if they were to meet an enemy, they would be able to win. They practiced how to shoot with bows and arrows. They practiced how to throw spears.

The knights practiced every day, and the king watched every day. He knew that Sir Roger was the best of his many knights, and so, he decided that

Sir Roger and Princess Juliana should get married someday. But, before a wedding could take place, Sir Roger would have to prove himself to be good enough to marry Princess Juliana. The king planned to send Sir Roger on a dangerous mission.

The king was very wise, but there was something that he did not know. Sir Roger and Princess Juliana already liked each other!

How did they get to know each other? There were many people running around the castle and the courtyard every day, all day long. How could Sir Roger and Princess Juliana meet without everyone in the castle knowing?

People ran around during the day, but they were very tired at night, and because they were tired, they slept very well.

It was in the middle of the night that Sir Roger and Princess Juliana met. They sat on the stones of the well under the old oak tree and talked. The more they talked, the more they liked each other. They didn't stay long because they didn't want anyone to see them.

One sunny, warm day, everyone in the kingdom was working in the fields. Some were planting crops, and some were watering their crops.

Suddenly, the Earth became dark. Something was covering the sun.

It was a giant dragon!

Chapter Two
The Biggest Dragon in the World!

No one had ever seen anything like this before. There were dragons living in caves in the mountains around the valley. People saw them from time to time, but they just stayed away from them. They were sort of like snakes; snakes often run away because they are more afraid of people than people are of them!

But no one in the kingdom had ever seen anything like this!

One of the jobs of a king is to protect his people. If there is ever a danger, everyone in the kingdom runs for the castle. If there are enemy soldiers, people run for the safety of the castle. From the castle, the knights can fight the enemy soldiers and drive them away. Then, the land will be safe again, and people can go back to their homes and their fields.

Because the people were very scared, they dropped their tools, their sacks, their lunches, and everything else around them. All they picked up were their babies.

And then everyone started to run to the foot of Castle Hill. The guards had already opened the wooden gates, because they too had seen the Earth grow dark; they too had looked up and seen the world's largest dragon. So they knew that all of the people of the kingdom would soon be coming to the castle for protection.

As the people starting to walk up the path, women carried their babies and young men helped the older people who were having trouble walking.

As they were reaching the top of the path, they could see that the guards had already opened the big wooden doors. Everyone happily shouted because now they could find safety and protection.

But their happiness came too soon. The dragon was not only big, but it was smart. It was watching how people were making their way up Castle Hill by following the path that wound around the steep cliffs.

Suddenly, the dragon swooped down from high above. It used its sharp claws and grabbed a man. The dragon carried the man away from Castle Hill.

Now the people were very scared. Not only had the dragon taken a man away, but now the people could see how ugly and dangerous the dragon was.

It was red, almost the color of blood. It had two huge wings, four legs with sharp claws, and a long tail. It had sharp spikes that ran from the back of its neck to the end of its tail.

And, as if that were not enough, its face was so scary that people looked away from it. It had more sharp spikes around its face and large, scary-looking golden eyes. People were afraid to look at its eyes because they were afraid they might die.

But, if you know anything about dragons, you know what the worst part is: fire! Dragons breathe fire, and because this was such a big dragon, everyone was worried about what the dragon might do.

The dragon was still carrying the man away from Castle Hill. People walked faster up the path in case the dragon came back.

The man had dropped everything when he had run to Castle Hill. But he always carried a knife with him. He waited until the dragon was flying low over the river, and he began to stab the dragon. The dragon had tough skin, but he didn't like what the man was doing, so he dropped him. Splash ... and right in the river! The man hid as fast as he could in the tall grasses that grew along the river.

He slowly made his way back to Castle Hill. He looked up into the sky often, and he tried to stay hidden as much as he could. Finally, he made it and went up the path as fast as he could.

By now, most of the people of the kingdom were safely inside the castle. The guards kept the big wooden doors open in case more people came up the path.

While all of this was happening, the king's men were taking their positions around the walls of the castle. At the top of the wall, there was a walkway that went the whole way around the castle wall. There were steps that led up to this walkway. There were also several towers. So you could walk up the steps, go along the walkway, and enter any of the towers.

These towers were important because they had long narrow holes in the walls. These were for the archers, the soldiers with bows and arrows. They could easily shoot arrows out of the narrow holes, but it was very difficult for anyone to shoot arrows through the holes into the towers.

The archers were ready, and the knights were ready. Some of the men who worked in the fields knew how to fight, so they were able to help, too.

The king was now too old and tired and weak to help fight such a huge enemy, so he asked his best knight, Sir Roger, to help to defend the kingdom. Sir Roger was happy to do this because he was a good knight, and he also wanted to marry Princess Juliana!

Everyone was now in place. People who were not fighters were hidden away in safe places. Even the chickens were put away. They didn't like this because they were used to running around the courtyard and doing whatever they wanted to do.

But something was wrong; it was too quiet. Everyone was listening. Where was the dragon? Had it gone away, or was it waiting for something?

But instead of hearing something, the people smelled something: fire!

The nasty dragon was flying all over the kingdom and setting everything on fire: the fields and crops, people's houses, horse stables -- everything it could find.

Suddenly, it swooped up to the top of Castle Hill and set the old oak tree on fire.

Chapter Three
A New Start

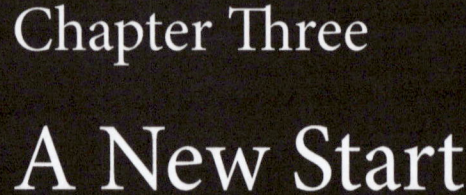

THE FIRST NECESSITY was to put out the fire in the old oak tree. It was not too hard to do. All of the knights and archers came down from the walkways and towers. They used buckets and got the water from the well. They started as soon as they could, so the fire was soon out.

Now the people of the kingdom were climbing the stairs to the walkway that surrounded the walls of the castle. They could not believe what they saw.

What had just moments before been a beautiful green valley was now ugly and black with grey smoke rising from the Earth.

"Our grains!"

"Our vegetables!"

"Our orchards!"

"Our vineyards!"

Everything was ruined. Some people were angry. Some people were sad and cried. One of them asked, "What are we going to do?"

"We'll just have to start again," answered a farmer.

While this was happening, Sir Roger quickly went and found the king.

"You majesty," said Sir Roger, "the people are very upset. It would help them so much if you could talk to them for just a short time."

So, the king agreed. By now, the old oak tree was safe, so the king sat on the side of the stone well. His queen sat on one side of him, and Princess Juliana sat on his other side.

Sir Roger had gone up the stairs to the walkway around the castle walls. He asked everyone to stay calm and come down to hear what the king had to say.

All of the people followed Sir Roger down to the courtyard. They gathered in front of the stone well where the king and his family sat. It was hard for the king to know what to say to so many people who had lost so much.

He said, "There is an old saying about good things rising up out of the ashes. I know it will be hard work, but I think you only have one choice: You must start again. Plow your fields, plant your seeds, water them well, and soon, our valley will be green again."

People were concerned about the orchards and the vineyards. "Take care of the fields first," said the king. "The trees and vineyards will grow again. And for your houses, work together to build them once again."

The people agreed. It was going to be hard work, and it was going to take some time, but they trusted their king.

Someone asked, "What if that bad old dragon comes back to our valley again?"

"Good question," answered the king. "I have a plan to take care of that dragon so that it will never do any damage or hurt anybody ever again."

Again, they trusted their king. They gathered up their babies and the young men helped the older people begin walking down the path from the top of Castle Hill to the bottom.

As the people reached the bottom, they were again saddened by all of the things they had lost. But they obeyed their king and started to make plans on what needed to be done first: plowing, planting, and watering.

As the last people went out of the wooden gate at the bottom of Castle Hill, the guards closed the gate. And the guards at the top of Castle Hill had already closed the big wooden doors to the castle.

People inside the castle walls began their jobs again, running around just like the chickens, which were finally taken out of their cages so that could run freely around the courtyard; they were very happy!

The king, the queen, and Princess Juliana were still quietly sitting on the stone well and watching all of the activity. One activity especially interested Princess Juliana: Sir Roger's practicing his sword fighting with another knight. She didn't care at all about the other knights; her eyes never left Sir Roger, and sometimes he would return her smile.

The king was old, but he noticed these looks. I wonder how long this has been going on? he asked himself. Sir Roger is the knight who I want to marry Princess Juliana. But is it possible that they already like each other?

The queen suddenly whispered to the king: "Are you thinking what I'm thinking?"

"What do you think I'm thinking?" the king whispered back to the queen.

"That a wedding is in the near future," answered the queen.

"Exactly," answered the king.

After the knights had finished practicing, the queen and the princess left the side of the stone well and went inside. The king continued to sit on the stone well's side until almost all the knights had left. Then he motioned for Sir Roger to come towards him.

"You are the best and bravest knight I have," started the king. "You have always served me well, and I want to reward you with the most valuable thing I have. But first, you must complete the most difficult task in the world."

"As you know, I am growing older and weaker each day," continued the king. "I need to find a good husband for my daughter. That is your reward; she is the most valuable thing I have. I feel that you and she could rule this kingdom and continue to do good things for all of the people."

Sir Roger waited while the king thought about what he wanted to say next. On one hand, Sir Roger was very happy about having Princess Juliana as his wife. On the other hand, he was a little nervous about the task that the king had mentioned.

"My wife and I both noticed how much you and Juliana like each other," said the king.

"It's true," said Sir Roger.

"So, you would like her as your wife?" asked the king.

"Yes, your majesty," answered Sir Roger.

"Here, then, is your task," said the king. "You must look for the dragon that burned our valley today, and you must destroy it."

Chapter Four

The Start of the Adventure

Sir Roger was shocked! He didn't say anything, but he couldn't help but think that this was going to be an impossible task. It could be a task from which he might not return.

"What do say, brave knight?" asked the king.

"You are my king," answered Sir Roger. "I must obey you and I must take on this task."

"Excellent," said the king. "When will you be able to start on your journey?"

"Tomorrow morning," answered Sir Roger.

The king said good night. He left the stone well and went inside.

Sir Roger bowed and

was just about ready to leave when he heard someone quietly call his name; it was Princess Juliana.

"What are you doing here?" Sir Roger asked.

"I wanted to hear what my father had to say to you," she answered.

"So now you know two things," said Sir Roger. "We are to be married, but first I must slay the giant dragon."

"Yes," said Princess Juliana. "I will think about you every day and wait for your return."

"But how I am to find this dragon?" asked Sir Roger.

"Here, take this," answered Princess Juliana.

"What is it?" asked Sir Roger.

"It is an ancient map that was given to me by an old witch many years ago," answered Princess Juliana.

Sir Roger opened it and looked at it.

"You see, here is our valley," said Princess Juliana, "and the map shows all the surrounding areas with mountains, streams, lakes, and, most importantly, dragon caves! If you use this, you are sure to find the giant dragon."

Sir Roger thanked her and slipped it into his pocket.

"Good luck," said Princess Juliana, "and see you soon!"

They said their goodbyes. Princess Juliana went back inside while Sir Roger walked over to the knights' quarters.

Sir Roger slept well but got up early to prepare everything he would need. He needed his weapons, of course, but he also needed to carry food and water. Luckily, he had an excellent and faithful horse to help him carry everything he needed.

The sun was just starting to rise in the east as Sir Roger crossed the blackened valley, but many people were already awake and working to make their fields green again.

He followed the course of the river. Soon, he started to notice that the land was no longer flat, and the water was a rushing stream that flowed into the river in the valley below.

Sir Roger had picked this direction because of something he had noticed on the ancient map that Princess Juliana had given him. There were many dragon caves around the mountains, but there was one cave that was much bigger than any of the other caves. He had an idea that this cave might be the home of the giant dragon.

He continued to follow the stream until he came to a spring. This spring was the source of the stream that flowed into the river that ran through the valley. Of course, there were other streams that flowed into the river; this was just one of several.

He filled his water containers because it was very fresh water, and his horse enjoyed the water, too.

Now, Sir Roger continued on his way up the slope above the spring. Soon, he reached the top of the mountain and looked all around. It was a beautiful day, and he wanted to think only about Princess Juliana, but he knew that there was danger ahead.

The first thing he heard as he started down the other side of the mountain was the sound of wolves. There were many dangers in the mountains, like wolves, bears, and even human bandits, so a knight always had to be prepared for whatever might come his way.

The noises of the wolves stopped. Sir Roger stopped his horse so he could listen. He couldn't hear anything, but his horse acted very nervous. Sir Roger pulled out his bow and arrow just in case.

And it was a good thing. A wolf jumped out from behind a rock and almost knocked Sir Roger off of his horse. But he was able to use his bow and arrow and continue on his way. Sir Roger was very happy that his horse was able to sense danger whenever he couldn't.

He and his horse continued down into the next valley. A black crow jumped off of a tree branch and flew down into the valley. This was a very small valley, and no one lived here. At least that was what Sir Roger thought.

But the next thing he knew, he was hearing a chuckling sound. He jumped off his horse to give it a rest and walked toward the chucking sound.

It was a wizard stirring something in a pot over a fire. This was in front of the hut where he lived.

Sir Roger did not want to scare the wizard, but he did not need to worry.

"I've been expecting you," said the wizard.

"Really?" asked Sir Roger.

"Oh yes," answered the wizard. "My friend told me you were coming."

Sir Roger looked over and saw the same crow that had seen earlier.

"This is your friend?" asked Sir Roger.

"He's my best friend," answered the wizard.

"Since you are a wizard, maybe you can help us," said Sir Roger.

"The giant dragon?" asked the wizard.

"How did you know that?" asked Sir Roger.

"I'm a wizard!" he answered. "And a very good one."

"So, can you help?" asked Sir Roger. "We have a very old map here that we thought might help us."

He showed the map to the wizard.

"Oh yes," said the wizard. "I know this map, and yes, it will help you. Just continue to the biggest of all the caves, and there you will find what you are looking for."

Sir Roger thanked the wizard for all of his help, and then, he turned around to look for his horse.

It was gone!

Chapter Five

The Magic Lake

A KNIGHT CANNOT look for a dragon without a horse, and his horse had been carrying everything the knight needed for his journey. He could not have wandered very far, thought Sir Roger. The wizard and I have only been talking for a short while.

The wizard!

Sir Roger heard the wizard chuckling again.

"What have you done with my horse?" asked Sir Roger.

The wizard continued to laugh.

Just then, Sir Roger heard the cry of a wolf. He looked around and noticed that a huge wolf was walking towards him. He got out his sword and was preparing to defend himself against an attack. Then, however, he noticed something very odd.

The wolf was carrying all of Sir Roger's things!

"What have you done?" he asked the wizard.

The wizard was rolling on the ground in laughter.

"You change him back into a horse this instant!" demanded Sir Roger.

"Okay, okay," said the wizard.

He got up from the ground and dusted himself off. He said a few magic words. Poof! The wolf changed back into the horse.

"Why did you do that to my horse?" asked Sir Roger.

"Not many people pass through my little valley," answered the wizard. "I don't often get the chance to have a little fun."

"Well thank you for the information," said Sir Roger. "I hope there is no trick in what you told us."

"No," said the wizard. "You can trust me. Everything I told you is true."

Sir Roger and his horse left the wizard and continued on their way through the small valley. Soon, they came to a small lake. The water was crystal clear.

Sir Roger walked towards the edge of the lake. It was perfectly calm. He looked down into the clear water. He thought he would see his reflection in the lake, but it was a magical lake.

Instead of seeing himself, he saw Princess Juliana! He could see her on the surface of the water.

"Juliana! Juliana!" cried Sir Roger. "Can you hear me? Can you see me?"

Sir Roger could tell that she was sitting on the edge of the stone well in the courtyard of the castle.

"Juliana!" he cried again.

This time, she looked around. Maybe she had heard his voice.

"It's me, Sir Roger," he said.

"I can hear you," she said. "Where are you?"

"Look into the well! Look into the well!" cried Sir Roger.

She was sitting on the stone well with her back to the water. She quickly turned around and put her hands on the stones at the edge of the well to support herself. She certainly did not want to fall into the well!

Just like Sir Roger at the magical lake, when Princess Juliana looked at the surface of the water, she expected to see herself. She had often looked into the well just to make sure her hair looked nice.

But, what a surprise! For the first time ever, she didn't see herself. She saw Sir Roger.

"Sir Roger!" she cried. "Is that really you?"

"Yes, it's me," he answered.

"Whatever are you doing down there in the well?" she asked. "I thought you were supposed to be off on a great adventure to slay the dragon and then come back and marry me! Are you not as brave as I thought you were?"

"Yes," answered Sir Roger. "I am as brave as ever. And I am not in the well like you think I am. I am far, far away in another valley. My horse and I came to this beautiful clear lake, and just before I started to take a drink, I looked down at the surface of the water expecting to see a reflection of myself. And, surprise: I saw you instead!"

Princess Juliana was amazed. "Do you mean that you can see me when you look in the lake?"

"Yes," answered Sir Roger.

"And I can see you in the surface of the water here in our well!" she said. "There must be very powerful magic at work."

Then she thought of something.

"Do you still have the map I gave you?" she asked.

"Yes," answered Sir Roger. "I keep it close to my heart, since it was you who gave it to me."

"Have you looked on the map at the valley where you are now?" Juliana asked him.

"I looked at it as we entered the valley," he answered.

"I was just curious if the magical lake is shown on the map," she said.

He pulled out the map and looked at it closely. He could see where he and his horse had climbed the mountain that separated the valley where the kingdom was found from the small valley where they had met the naughty wizard. He found the magical lake.

"I found it," he said to Juliana.

"Do you see anything else unusual?" she asked.

Sir Roger looked closely. And then he noticed something he hadn't seen before.

"I can't believe it!" he said.

"What do you see?" asked Juliana.

"There are tiny blue footprints that lead from Castle Hill in the valley, over the mountain, through the valley, and to the magical lake, right where we are standing now at the edge of the magical lake," answered Sir Roger.

"That's brilliant!" said Juliana. "Not only is it an ancient map, but it is a magical map. We have that wise old witch to thank for this amazing map."

Then she thought of something.

"It's great that it shows you where you have been," she said, "but it's too bad that it doesn't show you where you want to go."

Suddenly, a powerful blast of wind ripped the map from Sir Roger's hands. It went into the lake. He pulled it out.

Not only was it not wet, but now, it had tiny red footprints leading away from the magical lake.

"Juliana!" he cried.

But the spell had been broken. He could only see his own reflection in the water.

Chapter Six

The Mountain with the Surprise at the Top

After Sir Roger made this incredible discovery, he felt that his trip might be a little easier. All he needed to do was to follow the tiny red footprints on the magical map.

He could see where he and his horse were standing by the lake, and he could see that he needed to continue past the lake and out of the wizard's valley. At the far end of the valley, he could see that there was a quite high mountain that they would need to climb before they reached the caves of the dragons.

It was easy to see where his trip would end. Not only did he have the tiny red footprints to follow, but they suddenly stopped right in front of the biggest dragon cave of all!

Sir Roger took one last look at the magical lake hoping to see Juliana once more before he continued his way on his dangerous mission. But he could no longer see her, so with a little sadness, he left the lake.

He and his horse came to the end of the valley and now the high mountain stood before them. There was a layer of clouds surrounding the top of the mountain, so Sir Roger was not able to tell exactly how high this mountain was going to be. And he did know how challenging it was going to be!

He found a trail that looked as if it would lead them to the top of the mountain. He and his faithful horse slowly made their way up the mountain.

At the first it was not a steep climb: it was a gentle walk. But the further they continued up the mountain, the steeper it got. Not only did it get steeper, but the path became very rocky and he and his horse had to be careful so that they did not lose their footing and fall.

The other thing they noticed was that the plants were not the same as when they had started to walk up the mountain. There were no more flowers or shrubs, and eventually, there were no more trees. At this height, there were only little, low plants clinging to the rocks along the path.

Because of the layer of clouds, most of their journey up the mountain was foggy and misty. Sir Roger also noticed how cold it was getting. Soon, he was going to discover exactly what was happening.

The higher they climbed, the thinner the clouds became. They were no longer walking through mist and fog; they had cleared, and now, they could see what lay before them.

Snow!

This mountain peak was so high that there was snow at the top. There was also a huge glacier. Sir Roger certainly did not want to walk through snow and across a glacier, and although his horse was very faithful, if he could talk, he would have said to Sir Roger, "No way!"

But the tiny red footprints were pointing in that direction, so they had two choices. They could continue on their mission, or they could give up and return, defeated, to Castle Hill. They kept going because Sir Roger always had Juliana on his mind and in his heart.

To make it easier for his horse to walk in the snow, Sir Roger got off and walked in front, holding on to the horse's reins.

Above the clouds, it was a bright blue sunny day. After getting used to walking in the snow, Sir Roger actually started to enjoy the journey because of the beauty of the sky, the snow, the glacier, and the rocky peaks.

There was a small breeze blowing as they walked through the snow. Sir Roger began to notice that the wind was getting stronger and stronger. Soon the beautiful blue sky changed to a grey sky with huge storm clouds rolling across the top of the mountain. And within minutes, the pleasant journey changed into an ugly experience.

Where do you go when you are at the top of a mountain and a major snow storm arrives? You must look for some kind of protection where it is dry and warm.

Sir Roger wasn't sure what to do. The tiny red footsteps led the whole way to the rocky peak of the mountain. But with the heavy snow, it was getting hard to see where they were going.

They plodded through the snow, which was getting deeper and deeper each minute. Sir Roger could see that they were getting close to the rocky peak. He only hoped that there might be some kind of shelter, even if was in the crevices of the rocks or under an overhang.

By now, they could just barely see the rocky peak. They still had a way to go. Just then, they heard an extremely loud noise to the right of their path.

It was an avalanche!

Sir Roger was an excellent knight, but had had no training when it came to things like glaciers, snowstorms, and especially avalanches. All he knew was to continue straight up to the rocky peak and try to stay away from the dangerous and swiftly moving snow as it crashed its way down the side of the mountain.

His only hope was to get to the rocky peak and look for safety and shelter. There was a small break in the snowstorm, and he caught a quick glimpse of the rocky peak. He led his horse in that direction, hoping that they could find it in the snowstorm, which seemed to be getting worse.

Finally, they were close to the rocky peak. They could see several places where they could rest and be safe. Because his horse was big, Sir Roger looked for a big protected area. He found one and he and his horse went inside.

It seemed like the perfect place to rest.

Until they heard the growl of a mother bear!

Chapter Seven

Snow!

BEARS CAN be dangerous animals. But when a mother bear is protecting her cubs, watch out! She will do anything to protect her cubs, including any animals that come too close to her and her cubs.

So here was Sir Roger and his horse. They were finally out of the storm:

they had shelter; they had protection. But it was only one kind of protection: protection from the storm, not from a very angry and dangerous mother bear.

It was a very large protected area. Under other circumstances, animals could have shared the perfect place. But angry mother bears were not interested in sharing their spaces with other animals.

Sir Roger had only one choice: he and his horse had to gently and slowly back out of the protected area and once again go out into the raging snow storm. Fortunately, the mother bear did not follow them or try to hurt them.

Here they were again, out in the storm, looking for protection. They followed the rocks around to the right, looking closely for anything that might provide protection from the storm. After a long search, they finally found an overhang that would work for both Sir Roger and his horse.

But before they got too comfortable, Sir Roger looked around closely to make sure there were no dangerous animals inside. There were no other animals, so Sir Roger and his horse made themselves comfortable. They were both very tired and needed a long rest.

When Sir Roger work up, he noticed something new and different about their shelter.

Snow!

While they had been resting, the snowstorm had gotten much worse and had covered the entrance to their shelter. Sir Roger started digging in the snow to see how deep the covering was, and he soon saw daylight. The snowstorm had passed, and now, there was a beautiful blue sky again.

Because there had been a blue sky the previous day, and that blue sky had suddenly turned into a major snowstorm, Sir Roger did not want to stay very long on top of this mountain. He got his horse ready and soon they were on their way through a pass that led down to the other side of this high mountain.

He got out his map to make sure they were going in the right direction. They followed the tiny red footprints down the mountain and were soon out of the snow. Later they started to see the low plants, and then the shrubs and trees.

But they were not going down into another valley. The path now led along mountains, but much lower mountains than the snow covered mountain that they had just left. After all the snow and cold, it was a nice change and a pleasant walk across the mountains with their deep and ancient trees.

The tiny red footprints lead Sir Roger and his horse directly in front of a small cave. He knew it wasn't the cave of the giant dragon, but he was curious if all of the caves shown on the map were homes of dragons.

They stopped close to the entrance of the cave. Sir Roger slowly and quietly peeked inside of the cave. He could not see anything because it was quite dark in the cave. But he could smell something, and it did not smell very good.

It smelled like a combination of bad breath, burned bones, and other nasty things. It didn't take Sir Roger long to figure out that this was, in fact, the home of a dragon.

Just then, Sir Roger heard a noise inside. It was the sound of a dragon waking up and stirring. Sir Roger quickly stepped back from the entrance to the cave and got his bow and arrow ready.

However, he was too late! As fast as a bolt of lightning, the dragon flew out of the entrance to the cave and began circling, looking at what had disturbed its rest. He quickly spotted Sir Roger and his horse.

This dragon was young and small, so it did not fly as fast as other dragons. This was good for Sir Roger; it gave him the chance to practice on a smaller dragon before he met the giant dragon.

The small dragon flew up high. Then he came down towards Sir Roger as fast as he could. But Sir Roger was ready. He had his bow and arrow and hit the dragon before it got too close to him and his horse. It was a perfect shot: right through the dragon's heart. Sir Roger knew this was the best way to slay a dragon.

After this, Sir Roger and his horse continued to follow the tiny red footprints on the map. They walked along the mountain paths and came to another small cave. Sir Roger slowly walked towards the entrance of the cave.

Like the first cave, this cave was very dark, so he couldn't see anything. But he could hear lots of strange noises; he was sure this was not the home of a dragon. He took one more step toward the entrance of the cave.

Suddenly, there was a loud swoosh that knocked Sir Roger backwards. Thousands of large bats had been resting inside the cave. Sir Roger had disturbed them, and they had flown out of the cave because they were afraid of him!

So, now he knew that not all of the caves were the homes of dragons. He and his horse left the bat cave and continued to follow the tiny red footprints on the map. They were now getting close to the biggest cave of all.

Sir Roger hid his horse behind a rock. Then, he quietly looked inside the cave. It didn't smell very good, like the first dragon cave. But there was no noise. He walked further inside the cave.

Just then the giant dragon flew into the entrance of his cave.

Sir Roger was trapped!

At first, the giant dragon didn't know that Sir Roger was inside the cave. When he heard the giant wings flapping, Sir Roger had quickly made his way to the back of the cave and had hidden behind small large rocks.

There was not a lot that Sir Roger could do at this point; no matter how brave he was, and no matter how good he was at being a knight. After all, a giant dragon is a giant dragon!

For now, all he could do was to quietly wait and see if the giant dragon might go to sleep. Or maybe it might go out hunting again.

The giant dragon folded its wings behind its back and settled in for a nap. Sir Roger thought this might be his only chance to escape. He came out from behind the rocks where he had been hiding and tiptoed towards the dragon.

The giant dragon was sleeping with its head toward the entrance to his cave. Sir Roger was slowly and quietly walking up behind the giant dragon. He thought that he could safely pass along the side of the giant dragon and then sneak out of the front entrance to the cave.

Unfortunately, it was at this exact moment that Sir Roger's horse started to make noises outside. Instantly, the giant dragon was awake. The dragon didn't seem to notice Sir Roger, but the sound of a horse nearby meant an easy meal for the giant dragon. So, the dragon was out of the cave as fast as a bolt of lightning, eagerly in search of a meal.

The horse was well hidden behind some rocks, so the dragon was having a hard time finding him. In the meantime, Sir Roger had left the cave and snuck over to where his horse was hiding. There, behind the rocks, Sir Roger removed everything from the back of the horse. He tucked the magical map that Juliana had given him before he had left Castle Hill under his horse's reins.

"Go find Juliana," Sir Roger whispered to his horse. It would be a long, difficult trip for the horse, but he was good at remembering the way they had come. So, he just needed to retrace his steps back to Castle Hill.

Sir Roger patted his horse on his rear quarters, and the horse went off at a gallop. In the meantime, Sir Roger gathered up as many weapons that he could carry back to the giant dragon's cave. He had just gotten inside the cave when he heard the loud flaps of the giant dragon.

It was just about to enter the cave.

Sir Roger was now hiding again, behind the same rocks at the back of the cave. But now, he had his best equipment with him: his bow and arrow, his spear, his shield, his helmet, and many other things that knights use in battle.

Now, Sir Roger just had to wait for the best time to try to fight the giant dragon. But when would that time come?

While Sir Roger was waiting, trapped in the giant dragon's cave, his faithful horse was galloping as fast as he could. He had to go up over the snowy peak, down the other side, and into the wizard's valley.

The horse stopped briefly at the magical lake just to have a quick look, but he didn't see Juliana; he only saw himself.

He continued along the valley and avoided getting too close to the wizard because he had no time for any more tricks.

He climbed the next mountain and, on the way down the other side, saw the spring that he and Sir Roger had seen earlier. This was the source of one of the streams that fed the river that ran through the valley of the kingdom.

He was running along the river when he saw someone he recognized: it was Princess Juliana!

Why was she down at the river instead of up in the castle at the top of Castle Hill?

Sometimes princesses get bored sitting around castles coming their hair and looking at themselves in mirrors. So, on this day, Princess Juliana had gone down to the river to wash her hair in the river and to watch the ducks and swans.

Princess Juliana looked up and saw Sir Roger's horse. She was shocked and confused.

It was a good thing that no one else saw the horse. If anyone else had seen the horse, they would have reported it to the king. Then he would have needed to make arrangements for his army of knights and archers to go out and search for Sir Roger.

It was better this way. Princess Juliana already had an idea of where Sir

Roger was. Not only that, but she was also a very strong young woman: not just a strong body but a strong mind and a strong spirit, too. She was the kind of person who, once she had made up her mind to do something, could be stopped by nothing, and she always succeeded.

Princess Juliana climbed the back of the river and walked towards Sir Roger's horse. She instantly recognized the magical map she had given Sir Roger. It was still tucked under the horse's reins.

"What has happened to Sir Roger?" she asked the horse.

Of course, the horse could not answer, but it gestured that they needed to go as quickly as possible to save the trapped knight.

"Do you know that way?" she asked the horse.

The horse nodded and quietly whinnied.

Princess Juliana did not want people to know what was going on, so she decided not to go up to the top of Castle Hill to collect anything. She would just do the best she could with what she had.

Sir Roger had removed his horse's saddle. Fortunately, Princess Juliana had been taught how to ride bareback. Soon, they were on their way along the river towards the end of the valley.

Chapter Nine
Return to the Giant Dragon's Cave

A FEW PEOPLE looked up from their work in the fields. They were shocked to see Princess Juliana riding bareback away from Castle Hill along the river toward the far end of the valley.

"Where is she going?" they asked.

"I've never seen her ride along the river," someone said.

"And I've never seen her ride bareback," another person added. "She must be in a very big hurry, or maybe she's just having some fun."

She and Sir Roger's horse came to the end of the valley and started to climb up the first mountain. They stopped briefly for Princess Juliana and the horse to have a quick drink of fresh cold water at the spring along the way.

They reached the top of the small mountain and started to go down the other side in the wizard's valley. Juliana could not understand why the horse left the path of footprints on the map for a short time. But she couldn't ask him, so she decided that he knew what he was doing, and that there was some kind of danger that he was trying to avoid.

Shortly after that, they were on the path of the footprints again, and soon, they arrived at the magical lake.

"So this is the magical lake," said Juliana. She was looking at the map. She got down from the horse and looked at the surface of the lake. She hoped to see Sir Roger, but she only saw herself -- and she was rather pleased at what she saw!

She got on Sir Roger's horse again, and they continued on their way, following the footprints on the map. The horse knew what they were about to face, but Juliana did not.

They left the wizard's valley and started to climb up the high mountain.

The higher they climbed, the colder it got. I wish I had brought a coat along, Juliana thought to herself.

They climbed ever so high, above the forest trees and shrubs, until they could see the rocky peaks and the glacier. Fortunately, Princess Juliana was wearing shoes, so she walked along with the horse as they climbed higher and higher.

There was no stopping this time at the top of the mountain, especially at the mother bear's den! They reached the top of the mountain and then began to go down the other side. Princess Juliana was nearly frozen, so it was with great relief that they passed beyond the snow and soon began to see the mountain trees and shrubs. The air started to become warmer.

Juliana and the horse passed by the first cave where Sir Roger had slain the dragon. So now Juliana was sure they were going in the right direction. Then they came to the bat cave. As they walked past the cave, the bats heard them and, as before, thousands of bats flew out of the cave because they were afraid of Juliana and the horse.

And now they were getting close to the third cave, the biggest cave for the biggest dragon.

Juliana followed the horse to the place behind the rocks where Sir Roger had first hidden him. The horse's saddle and other things were still here, so Juliana figured out that Sir Roger had his weapons with him.

She asked the horse to stay hidden while she went closer to the entrance of the cave. It was so dark and she could not see.

But just then the giant dragon sneezed. And when it sneezed, it blew a stream of fire across the cave and out of the entrance. Juliana was standing just to the side of the entrance. Her gown caught one fire, but just a little bit, and she was able to put it out quickly. Rats, she thought, my best gown.

She had to think for a while. The giant dragon had to be slain. Sir Roger had to escape. She didn't want to do anything that would put his life or her life in danger. And the horse: the faithful horse had to be saved too.

Suddenly Juliana came up with a plan!

There was a long rope back with the saddle and other things where the horse was waiting. She grabbed the rope and quietly went back to the entrance of the cave. She tied one end of the rope to a big rock on the left side of the entrance to the cave. Then, she tiptoed across to the other side of the entrance. Here she pulled the rope tight and tied it to a big rock on the right side.

The giant dragon was asleep, but Sir Roger had been watching what Princess Juliana had been doing. He figured that her idea was to trip the giant dragon as it started to fly out of the cave. Hopefully, it would fall backwards, and then, it was up to Sir Roger to use his weapons to slay the giant dragon.

Everything was ready to go. Sir Roger had his weapons ready, and Juliana was standing outside of the entrance to the giant dragon's cave.

Just then, Sir Roger dropped his spear. It made a loud rattle as it fell to the ground. The dragon woke up and was just about to breathe fire on Sir Roger when Juliana screamed at the top of her lungs. This distracted the giant dragon.

As he was getting ready to fly out of the cave and grab Juliana, she ran to one side of the cave. Just as planned, the dragon tripped and fell over backwards.

Sir Roger threw his spear with all of his might at the giant dragon's chest, but the dragon was still alive. Sir Roger jumped on top of the dragon's chest and thrust his sword right into the heart of the giant dragon.

That did it! The giant dragon would never bother the kingdom again.

But where was Juliana? She had disappeared after having screamed.

After she had screamed, and the giant dragon had lunged towards her, Sir Roger had been busy slaying the dragon, so he hadn't noticed what had happened to Princess Juliana.

She had fallen over backwards and, thanks to her best gown, she was now dangling part of the way down a cliff.

Sir Roger quickly untied the rope from one of the two big rocks and lowered himself down to save Juliana. She grabbed hold of him, after untangling her gown from the sharp rock, and he pulled them both up to safety.

He gathered all of his weapons, and they walked to his horse, which was still faithfully waiting for him.

"You and Princess Juliana saved my life," Sir Roger said to Juliana and to the horse. "I think we'll have to include him in our wedding plans!"

They loaded everything onto the horse and began their long journey back home to Castle Hill. After the caves, the snowy peaks, the wizard's valley with the magical lake, and the final mountain, they arrived at the valley of the kingdom.

But what a surprise they had when they first saw the valley! It was green again! It was no longer black!

Sir Roger and Princess Juliana asked some people in the fields what had happened.

"Yesterday, in the middle of the afternoon, suddenly everything turned green," answered one worker.

"It's a miracle," said another.

Sir Roger and Princess Juliana figured it out. When the giant dragon was slain, the fields, orchards, and vineyards all returned to their healthy green state.

Now it was time for Sir Roger and Princess Juliana to go up to the top of Castle Hill. They both knew that everyone would be happy that the giant dragon had been slain; but they were not so sure that the king would be happy that Princess Juliana had put herself in such great danger.

They walked across the courtyard and saw the king and queen sitting on the edge of the stone well. They were so happy to see Sir Roger and their daughter, but the king was a little unhappy.

"Where have you been?" he asked his daughter.

"I've been on a little adventure," she answered.

"But where?" asked the king.

"Sir Roger and I slew the giant dragon," answered Juliana. "And that is why the valley is green again.

"You helped Sir Roger to slay the giant dragon?" asked the king.

"Yes," answered Juliana.

"I was trapped in the dragon's cave," explained Sir Roger. "My horse came back here to find Juliana. Then she helped to trip the dragon so that it would fall. When it fell backwards, I was able to slay it."

"What has happened to your beautiful gown?" asked the queen.

"Oh nothing," answered the princess. "I just fell backward down the side of a cliff, and thank goodness, I was wearing this gown because it is made of strong fabric and it got caught on a sharp rock."

The queen looked like she was about to faint.

"But then Sir Roger came down on a rope and saved me," said Juliana. "But I will be needing a new gown. Hopefully, it will be white."

The king now turned to Sir Roger. "Sir Roger: you have completed your task. You have slain the giant dragon: it will never hurt us again. Because of this brave deed, I give you my daughter's hand in marriage."

Now the whole kingdom knew the story of how Juliana had saved Sir Roger and how Sir Roger had slain the dragon and had saved Juliana.

Plans for the wedding began almost immediately. Princess Juliana did, in fact, get a new gown, and it was, in fact, white!

On the day of the wedding, the king and the queen stood in front of the stone well under the old oak tree in the center of the courtyard. Sir Roger and Princess Juliana were married in front of the king and queen, and Sir Roger's faithful horse stood nearby.

After the ceremony, there was a huge feast with plenty of food for everyone in the kingdom to eat. When everyone had finished eating, it was time to say goodbye to Sir Roger and Princess Juliana. However, it was not to be for long: just a short visit to another nearby valley.

Sir Roger helped Juliana get up on his horse, and then he jumped on the front of the horse. With the whole kingdom cheering, Sir Roger and Juliana rode out of the courtyard and down to the bottom of Castle Hill.

They lived happily ever after, and the valley was always green.

The End

Edward Alan Kurtz

About the Author

EDWARD is an American writer.

He specializes in writing works of fiction and non-fiction for children, as well as travel books and articles.

Ed was born in Pennsylvania and completed several university degrees.

He lived for many years in Honolulu, Hawaii, and now lives and writes in Thailand.

Previous books:

- Max and The Map
- Christmas in the Forest
- Springtime in the Forest
- Summertime in the Forest

~ • ~

www.ingramcontent.com/pod-product-compliance
Lightning Source LLC
Chambersburg PA
CBHW042036100526
44587CB00030B/4454